The Future Starts Now!

Mike Beaumont

Salt and Light Ministries

Series Editor: Mike Beaumont
Oxford, UK

Cover design: James Kessell Design (01844 260429)

Contents

Foreword

"What is hidden in the roots will be revealed in the shoots."

This has been one of the lifelong principles by which I have sought to live and build. Experience tells us that what the roots of the plant are like, and what they feed on, determines what sort of fruit grows; where the foundations of a building are shaky, time and disaster will reveal it; where the most simple flaws are not spotted, dreadful disasters can follow – as when a basic defect in the fuel system of the Challenger space craft cost the lives of seven brave astronauts.

So it is with people. What we believe in our hearts will eventually determine how we live, how we build and what we end up with.

This "Roots and Shoots" series is not so much an attempt to define the distinctives of our family of churches, but rather to ensure that all our beliefs and practices are firmly rooted in the Scriptures.

Many people have asked us over the years: "Who are you and what do you believe?" While our structure may appear to be somewhat nebulous, nevertheless the understanding of our common beliefs needs to be clear and unambiguous.

We are a family of churches that believe we are to be "sons of the kingdom" sown into God's earth. The key that transforms "the word of the kingdom" into "sons of the kingdom" is *understanding* (Matthew 13:23). In the Lord's first parable of the kingdom (the Sower), the 'word' of the kingdom – the seed – when properly received and understood produces fruit. In the second parable of the kingdom (the Weeds), we discover that the fruit has become the seed, and that the seed is "the sons of the kingdom". The word, bearing fruit, producing seed as sons of the kingdom, planted in the world! That is our prayer for this series of books.

Barney Coombs

Introduction

I well remember my first visit to Merryfield House in Witney, Oxfordshire. It was for one of the early leaders' conferences within the Salt and Light family of churches in the UK, and there were just twenty-five or so of us gathered there. I was 'the new boy' and felt somewhat overwhelmed by it all; but the theme for the conference was 'The Kingdom of God' – surely a safe and easy enough topic. But as I listened intently to the teaching by the visiting speaker that week, I soon realised that I didn't have the faintest idea what he was going on about! How could this be? I had only recently graduated from Bible College!

I went home from that conference with mixed emotions – annoyed, frustrated – and yet provoked. Something was clearly missing in my understanding. Lectures at Bible College had *covered* the topic, but had clearly not *revealed* it. Even reading over my college notes again didn't seem to help! Over the coming months, however, the penny slowly 'began to drop' – probably more as a result of God's *revelation* than my *investigation*. But then, that is what the kingdom is like.

In fact, that is what everything is like where God is concerned! *Revelation* is always the key. That's what turned things round for Peter when he suddenly saw who Jesus was: "Blessed are you, Simon son of Jonah, for this was not revealed to you by man, but by my father in heaven." (Matthew 16:17) Study, while tremendously helpful and important, will never 'get us there' on its own. It needs *revelation* adding to it; and that's what began to change my understanding of the kingdom.

So, by all means read about the kingdom: study it; explore it; ask your questions about it. Indeed, not to do is just plain silly, when Jesus says it is the one thing we are to seek after more than anything else in life (Matthew 6:33)! But as you do so, cry out, above all things, for God to bring *revelation* to you, so that you might *see* it, and then *understand* it, and so, consequently, *live* it. For that is what the kingdom is all about.

Chapter 1

A Coming King and a Trampled Field

How easy it is to use a word without really understanding it. In the week I wrote this, the Head of our church Senior School had been to a secular education conference that was buzzing with the latest schemes and requirements. "They all seemed to be talking so knowledgeably," he said, "but I'm convinced that most of them were talking without having the faintest idea of what they were actually saying!" But in the good tradition of the Emperor's clothes, they kept on talking anyway, lest anyone noticed they were naked.

Of course, we would never do that, would we? I often wonder! It's not unusual to hear Christians talking about 'the kingdom': kingdom principles, kingdom men, kingdom women, kingdom values, kingdom finances. But what *is* the kingdom?

We Know the Answer!

The Jews of Jesus' day thought they knew the answer to that question, for they had a long tradition about it that ran through their Scriptures. They had no doubt, first and foremost, that God alone was King: "the King of glory" (Psalm 24:7-10), "the great King over all the earth" (Psalm 47:1-9), "the great King above all gods" (Psalm 95:3). They had no doubt that, as such, "the LORD has established his throne in heaven, and his kingdom rules over all" (Psalm 103:19), that this throne was at the centre of all things (e.g. Isaiah 6:1; Ezekiel 1:26; Daniel 7:9-14), and that all things were therefore ultimately under his control. Even the greatest empires of mankind, even those that now resisted his purposes, would ultimately crumble before his kingdom (e.g. Daniel 2:31-45) and every knee would bow before his throne (Isaiah 45:23). There was no hint here of any 'cosmic dualism' – a battle between good and evil in which the outcome might go either way (rather like in the Star Wars films!). The King was enthroned, so the outcome was assured; his throne would indeed "last for ever and ever" (Psalm 45:6).

When Messiah Comes ...

The outworking and establishing of this rule of God on the earth would come about, the Prophets assured them, through Messiah. He would destroy all evil (which, in current Jewish understanding, meant everyone who wasn't a Jew) and establish his righteous reign on earth, focused in Jerusalem (e.g. Psalm 2:1-6; Isaiah 9:6-7; 32:1; Jeremiah 23:5-6; Daniel 7:13-27; Micah 4:1-7). And everything in the garden would then be wonderful, as though Eden itself had been restored (e.g. Isaiah 11:6-9).

By the time of Jesus, the focus of this thinking was the Roman Empire, under whose iron grip, along with much of the known world, the nation of Israel lay. Rome would be the great enemy that would be overthrown, as Messiah raised up an army to remove these defiling pagans once and for all.

But Israel was split on the matter: in one corner of the 'boxing ring' were those who didn't want to shake the status quo for fear of losing their political influence (like the Sadducees); in another corner were the 'Freedom fighters' of the day (like Simon 'the Zealot' who would become a different sort of revolutionary when he became a disciple of Jesus); in another were the godly, like Simeon who was "waiting for the consolation of Israel" (Luke 2:25) and Anna who was "looking forward to the redemption of Jerusalem" (Luke 2:38); and in the final corner were the ordinary people who felt their life would probably not change greatly whoever came out on top.

It was into this setting that Jesus came, proclaiming the certainty of the coming of the kingdom – but a kingdom of quite a different nature from that which they had come to expect.

A Trampled Field

A key to understanding how Jesus saw the kingdom is found in one of his shortest parables about it:

"The kingdom of heaven is like treasure hidden in a field. When a man found it, he hid it again, and then in his joy went and sold all he had and bought that field." (Matthew 13:44)

Two fields or one?

First of all, let's get one issue out of the way. Over the years I have heard sermons and read books explaining the difference between 'the kingdom of heaven' (the term used by Matthew) and 'the kingdom of God' (the term used by Mark and Luke). Two different words – two different kingdoms, quite obviously; one future, one present; one spiritual, one physical, so the argument goes. In other words, Jesus didn't quite get it right in the parable; there are two fields, not one!

Nothing could be further from the truth. The two different terms are completely synonymous, for they are used in exactly the same teaching or setting by the different gospel writers. For example, Matthew says the kingdom of *heaven* is like a mustard seed (Matthew 13:31), while Mark and Luke say the kingdom of *God* is like a mustard seed (Mark 4:30-31; Luke 13:18-19). Clearly they are not referring to two different kingdoms or even to two different aspects of the same kingdom; they are talking about the same thing in the same context. The explanation is quite simple: Matthew was writing for a Jewish readership, and hence he followed the convention of the time of not using the name of 'God' directly, as this was seen as irreverent. Being sensitive to his readers' background and scruples, he therefore speaks of 'the kingdom of *heaven*' (a common phrase used instead of God's name at the time) rather than 'the kingdom of *God*'. So we don't need to take on board any notions of two separate kingdoms. The kingdom is one field, not two.

Hidden treasure

To a people who were expecting the kingdom of God to come in the form of a Messiah on a white horse leading a mighty army, Jesus' teaching must have sounded strange indeed. He said that the kingdom of God was "near" (e.g. Matthew 4:17), that it was "upon you" (Matthew 12:28), that it was "among you" or "in your midst" or "within your grasp" (more likely renderings of the phrase "within you" in Luke 17:21), that it was "forcefully advancing" (Matthew 11:12). All of these clearly implied that the kingdom was already here. And yet so many didn't see it! So where was it? It was, Jesus said, "like treasure hidden in a field" (Matthew 13:44).

Now the thing about hidden treasure is that it is as near to the person who found it as the person who missed it! No doubt the farmer had ploughed that field many times; no doubt children had played in it often; no doubt travellers had cut across it many times – perhaps for generations. And yet they had all missed the treasure. They had walked over it, but not known it was there. *That's* what the kingdom is like, said Jesus. So near! And yet, without revelation, without 'finding it', so far. God has hidden it; yet he wants us to find it. But to find it, he says that we will need to look, and we will need to give everything to the process and to the consequence. The reason so many of Jesus' contemporaries missed it – and the reason so many have missed it ever since! – is because they were looking for the *wrong thing* in the *wrong place*, and so came up with the *wrong answer*.

So, then, what is the kingdom? It's to this that we turn in the next chapter.

Chapter 2

The Nature of the Kingdom

In the previous chapter we saw how many of Jesus' contemporaries missed the kingdom because they were looking for the wrong thing. In this chapter we want to look at how Jesus saw it. We can sum up his understanding of the kingdom of God in three simple phrases: rule before realm; now before then; 'this-worldly' before 'that-worldly'. Let's look at each in turn.

Rule before Realm

When we use the word 'kingdom' we tend to think of a place – like 'the United Kingdom'. Now while the New Testament word ('basileia' in Greek) can mean that, it is not the primary thrust of its meaning. To capture its feel we need to translate it as 'rule', 'sovereignty', or 'dominion'. It is not so much the place ruled, as the act of ruling. The kingdom is, then, a rule before a realm. One day it will be a realm – a definable 'place'; but not yet!

The kingdom as a 'rule'

The fact that Jesus did not see the kingdom in terms of geographical location comes out in much of his teaching. So, for example, "If I drive out demons by the finger of God, then the kingdom of God has come to you" (Luke 11:20). But the Romans were still there! So how can it have come? Later in Luke we read this: "Once having been asked by the Pharisees when the kingdom of God would come, Jesus replied, 'The kingdom of God does not come with your careful observation, nor will people say, "Here it is" or

"There it is", because the kingdom of God is within [or, better, *among*] you'"
(Luke 17:20-21).

This second saying begins to reveal something of the present nature of
the kingdom. It is not *geographical*, it is *spiritual*. You can't see it, but it's
real; you can't locate its borders, but it can cross all borders and not be
intimidated by any of them – even those wretched Roman invaders.

An illustration might help here. We are accustomed these days to big
multi-national corporations, like Ford or Microsoft. Their budgets are often
far bigger than that of many nations, their influence far more widespread,
and they can operate irrespective of national borders. Limited by no particular
government, extending beyond many governments, they can affect (if not
control!) what governments do. That's what the kingdom of God is like! For
the moment, you can't define it or locate it in time or space; but it's *there*, it's
real, and it's influencing. Wherever that rule of the King is received, things
begin to change. Lives get cleaned up; families are rebuilt; businesses start to
operate righteously; economic systems become more healthy; nations start
doing things the right way; and the blessing of God inevitably follows.

The kingdom is here right now! That was the startling message that
Jesus brought; that's what so many of his contemporaries couldn't work out;
that's what so many Christians have not yet seen. Yet the more you look at
Jesus' teaching, the more obvious it becomes. "The field is …" What?
'Heaven' when I get there one day? No! "The field is *the world,*" Jesus said
(Matthew 13:38) when explaining the parable of the weeds to his disciples.
It's here! That's why so many of his kingdom parables begin with, "The
kingdom of heaven *is* like …", *not* "The kingdom of heaven *will be* like … ".
The kingdom is here because Jesus is here!

And yet there's more!

The kingdom as a 'realm'

While the kingdom is not yet a realm – that is, while it does not yet have
geographical territory and boundaries as other realms do – it *will* be a realm
one day. In fact, there will be a time when God's kingdom will be the only
realm that is left and when all other realms and nations will have yielded
before it, just as Daniel saw in his vision of the statue. The statue, representing

the nations of the world, will crumble under the blow of the Messianic rock that strikes it:

"A rock was cut out, but not by human hands. It struck the statue on its feet of iron and clay and smashed them. Then the iron, the clay, the bronze, the silver and the gold were broken to pieces at the same time and became like chaff on a threshing floor in the summer. The wind swept them away without leaving a trace. But the rock that struck the statue became a huge mountain and *filled the whole earth*" (Daniel 2:34-35). (See also his visions in Daniel 7:1-27; 8:1-26.)

At last the cry will then go up, when the final trumpet of human history is sounded, that "the kingdom of the world has become the kingdom of our Lord and of his Christ, and he will reign for ever and ever" (Revelation 11:15).

Our ultimate destination is not 'heaven'. Heaven is but a most beautiful 'waiting room' (quite unlike those at railway stations!) where we enjoy the presence of God until the return of Jesus to *this* earth, when at last "the *earth* will be full of the knowledge of the LORD as the waters cover the sea" (Isaiah 11:9). The book of Revelation ends, not with our floating on clouds in *heaven* playing harps or even singing 'holy, holy, holy', but with a description in beautiful pictorial form of God's kingdom coming down onto the *earth*.

"Then I saw a new heaven and a new earth, for the first heaven and the first earth had passed away, and there was no longer any sea. I saw the Holy City, the new Jerusalem, coming down out of heaven from God, prepared as a bride beautifully dressed for her husband. And I heard a loud voice from the throne saying, 'Now the dwelling of God is with men, and he will live with them. They will be his people, and God himself will be with them and be their God. He will wipe every tear from their eyes. There will be no more death or mourning or crying or pain, for the old order of things has passed away' " (Revelation 21:1-4).

At last, the rule will be a realm! But there's lots to be done before then!

Because the kingdom of God is a 'rule' before a 'realm', two other things follow:

'Now' before 'Then'

The kingdom is not something we have to wait for as we sit around twiddling our thumbs. Its coming on the earth in all its fullness will definitely be a 'then' – something for the future; but there's a 'now' to be experienced and enjoyed long before that.

The kingdom is 'now'

Many of Jesus' parables and teachings bring home the fact that the kingdom is not something just to be waited for, but that it is already here, because Jesus is here. That was the point of his reading from Isaiah in the synagogue in Nazareth:

"The Spirit of the Lord is on me, because he has anointed me to preach good news to the poor. He has sent me to proclaim freedom for the prisoners and recovery of sight for the blind, to release the oppressed, to proclaim the year of the Lord's favour." (Luke 4:18-19)

Freedom is here because I am here, Jesus was saying. To authenticate this, he then went on to heal the sick, cast out demons, and raise the dead – all things that have to yield in the presence of the king! On one occasion, having freed a mute man from an evil spirit, Jesus said, "If I drive out demons by the finger of God, then the kingdom of God *has come* to you" (Luke 11:20). In other words, it's here – right now!

The parables of the kingdom in Matthew 13 also reflect this 'here and now' dimension. The sower's seed is already being scattered and is starting to bring forth a return (vv3-23); the wheat is already growing among the weeds (vv24-30); the mustard seed is planted and steadily growing (vv31-32); the yeast is already in the dough and doing its work (v33); the treasure and the pearls can be found right now (vv44-45); the net is already gathering its fish (vv47-50). The kingdom is truly 'among us'.

The kingdom is 'then'

But Jesus also makes it clear that we don't have everything yet! Even some of the parables to which we have just referred have a future dimension in them also (e.g. Matthew 13:30, 40-43, 49). Jesus' teaching about the end times and his return in Matthew 24, and his parables in Matthew 25 about the need to be ready in the light of that return, distinctly point us to a future aspect of the kingdom that is yet to be revealed. Only when he returns will all obstructions to the kingdom be removed (Revelation 20:7-15) and the kingdom at last be revealed in all its glorious fulness.

How can it be 'now' before 'then'?

The future aspect of the kingdom was not difficult for Jesus' contemporaries to grasp; what they struggled with was how on earth it could have a 'now' dimension.

If you look at rock faces, the different strata of rock will often be clearly visible, layer upon layer. Sometimes you can even see where one layer has pushed hard against another during movements of the earth's crust, and in fact has pushed so hard that one layer has 'slipped over' the top of the other layer. That's rather what it is like with God's kingdom. With the coming of Jesus, the future age has pushed hard into the present age and has 'overlapped' it.

As believers, we now live in a world of 'overlap' or 'breakthrough'. Our life is firmly rooted in the present, for this is the age and the world in which we must live; but the future has overlapped our present, just like those rock strata, and has broken through into it, so that right now we can begin to experience something of the life and power of 'the age to come'. Which leads us on to our third point:

'This Age' before 'That Age'

We don't have to 'wait until we get to heaven' to start experiencing the life that God has for us! The kingdom is here – in *this* world! – because Jesus himself is here. It is to be found in this present age before it is to be found in the future coming age.

The kingdom is of 'this age'

Again and again Jesus used various images to bring home the kingdom's presence and nearness to us right now, here in this age and world:

From that time on Jesus began to preach, "Repent, for the kingdom of heaven is *near*." (Matthew 4:17)

"But if I drive out demons by the Spirit of God, then the kingdom of God has *come upon you*." (Matthew 12:28)

"When Jesus saw that he [a teacher of the law] had answered wisely, he said to him, 'You are *not far* from the kingdom of God.' " (Mark 12:34)

"Do not be afraid, little flock, for your Father has been pleased to *give you* the kingdom." Luke 12:32)

"The kingdom of God does not come with your careful observation, nor will people say, 'Here it is,' or 'There it is,' because the kingdom of God is among you." (Luke 17:20-21)

Near – upon – not far – given – among; all this is the language of immediacy and closeness, not of waiting for something yet to come; of a 'this age and this world' kingdom, not just a 'that age and that world' one.

Yet though the kingdom is to be found and expressed in this world, it is not to be established by worldly means. That's why Jesus said to Pilate at his trial, "My kingdom is not of this world. If it were, my servants would fight to prevent my arrest by the Jews. But now my kingdom is from another place" (John 18:36). That's why Peter had been told to put his sword away in the Garden of Gethsemane (John 18:11), for the kingdom was to be established not by a sword, but by a cross.

This idea of the presence *now* of the *future* kingdom comes out in the word for 'eternal' in the New Testament, which literally means 'of the age (to come)'; that is, of God's 'age' or 'dimension', as opposed to man's. When Jesus promised 'eternal life', he wasn't so much thinking of never-ending life (though it included that); he was promising life that is characteristic of God's dimension being available to us right here and now; yet life that was so powerful that, when our years are over, it would burst through the doors of death and continue in the life to come in even fuller expression.

The treasure really is hidden in the field right now; and that's why it's worth giving everything for (Matthew 13:44). But once again, there is so much more to come!

The kingdom is 'that-worldly'

While Jesus taught clearly that the kingdom was present, he also taught that there was an aspect of it still to come. We don't have everything yet! The 'overlapping' kingdom is certainly here, but it is limited by its co-existence with this present world order. Only at his return, Jesus said, would this world be 'wrapped up' so that all that remained would be the kingdom (e.g. Revelation 11:15).

A number of Jesus' parables underline this future aspect of the kingdom; for example, the weeds (Matthew 13:24-30, 36-43), the net (Matt 13:47-50), the workers in the vineyard (Matt 20:1-16), the wedding banquet (Matt 22:1-14), the ten virgins (Matt 25:1-13), the talents (Matt 25:14-30), the sheep and the goats (Matt 25:31-46).

By and large Christians have done quite well at grasping the 'that-worldly' dimension of the kingdom. The belief that Jesus will come for us again at death and take us to our heavenly home (e.g. John 14:1-3); that those who die 'in Christ' are secure in heaven (e.g. Revelation 7); that Christ will come again one day on the clouds, with all the saints, to gather those still alive so that we shall always be with him together (e.g. 1 Thessalonians 4:13-18); that the future kingdom will be a wonderful place, free from all wrongs (e.g. Revelation 21 and 22); all these things have been firm aspects of orthodox Christian future hope over the centuries.

In fact, if anything, the church has veered too much this way. Much of this way of thinking is rooted in the Greek mindset that the western world developed, rooted in the philosophy of Plato, with its sharp division between the spiritual, eternal realm and the physical, earthly realm. Throughout church history, this false division was increasingly intensified, and became an unwitting foundation even of much twentieth century evangelical theology. In fact, much to our shame, it was the liberal theologians who first began to rediscover the message of the kingdom.

Continuity, yet Discontinuity

The kingdom of God is here; yet the kingdom of God is coming. It is rule before realm; now before then; of *this* age and world before *that* age and world. Keeping these different aspects in balance is not always easy, and the tendency is to veer all too easily in one direction or the other, depending on our theology or our background. Yet Jesus says the kingdom is about *both* aspects and so we must seek to hold on to both.

There is, on the one hand, a continuity between the two aspects; it is not a *different* kingdom that is coming one day; it is *this* present kingdom, but in all its fulness. There is clear continuity between the two. This is what makes it worthwhile giving ourselves to the kingdom *now*; to sowing the kingdom *now*; to planting kingdom seed in the family, or in the workplace, or in the nation *now*. For what is planted *now* will come to fruition *then*. That is why it is so silly to adopt a 'We can't do very much, so hold the fort until Jesus comes!' mentality.

But equally, there is a discontinuity between the two aspects; a 'break' that is needful. For there are some things about the kingdom that we will never be able to see in this life and this age. Paul put it like this: "I declare to you, brothers, that flesh and blood cannot inherit the kingdom of God" (1 Corinthians 15:50). In other words, as well as continuity, there is discontinuity. *This* age is going to have to yield to *that* age; the present is going to have to yield to the future; imperfection is going to have to yield to perfection; the partial is going to have to yield to the complete (1 Corinthians 13:9-10). There are some things that we will just never see until Jesus himself returns at the end of the age, when the 'continuity' of the kingdom will be transformed into its next phase by the 'discontinuity' of the return of Jesus. Like a child in the womb being brought into the world, the kingdom will be brought into the full expression of all that God has been preparing. But, like the child in the womb, not everything should be left for the birth! The return of Jesus is not an excuse for sitting back and thinking that we can do nothing because we can't do everything.

The kingdom is surely coming; but the kingdom is surely here. So, what makes this kingdom 'tick'? It is to this that we will turn in the next chapter.

Chapter 3

The Heart of the Kingdom

If you really want to know what makes something 'tick' then you need to get right to the heart of it. Businesses express how they 'tick' in their values and mission statements. But far more insightful than words on paper is seeing 'the man at the top'. What he (or she) is like will make the company what it is (or isn't!). An example of this is Richard Branson whose 'Virgin' companies are all reflections of him, his style, and his basic approach to life.

So, if we want to know what the kingdom of God is like, then we will look at the God of the kingdom. This booklet cannot possibly cover everything that there is to say about God! (However, for an excellent overview, see Tony Gray's "What is God like?" in this series.) But there are three things about God in particular that are especially relevant for our study; three things that you find at the very heart of the kingdom.

A King!

As we saw in Chapter 1, the conviction that "the Lord is King!" lies at the very heart of biblical faith. Psalm 47 is a good summary of this:

"Clap your hands, all you nations;
   shout to God with cries of joy.
How awesome is the LORD Most High,
   the great King over all the earth!
He subdued nations under us,
   peoples under our feet.
He chose our inheritance for us,

the pride of Jacob, whom he loved.   *Selah*

God has ascended amid shouts of joy,
   the LORD amid the sounding of trumpets.
Sing praises to God, sing praises;
   sing praises to our King, sing praises.

For God is the King of all the earth;
   sing to him a psalm of praise.
God reigns over the nations;
   God is seated on his holy throne.

The nobles of the nations assemble
   as the people of the God of Abraham,
for the kings of the earth belong to God;
   he is greatly exalted."

Four basic convictions run through the Scriptures about this king:

The King's throne is central

We have seen how this is reflected in many places in the Old Testament; but let's look at an example from the New Testament. John, exiled on Patmos during a time of unparalleled persecution against the Christians, had a revelation from God to help him make sense of all that was happening around him and to help him understand what would happen in the future. What towers over every scene in that revelation is *the throne of God*. In fact, there are thirty-eight references to God's throne in the book of Revelation. The throne is where the vision starts (Revelation 1:4) and ends (22:3); the throne is where all worship is focused (4:1-11); the throne is where the one who holds the scroll of human history is seated (5:1-14); the throne is where all judgment comes from (6:1-17); the throne is where the faithful dead are gathered as they wait for the end (7:1-17); the throne is the place before which all prayer arises (8:3-4); the throne is the secure abode of the ascended Christ until his return (12:5); the throne is the source of the judgments poured out upon the earth (16:15-21); the throne is the place of final judgment, before which all men must appear (20:11-15); the throne lies at the heart of God's re-created order at the end of time (21:1-4; 22:1-5).

What is at the centre of everything? The throne! What is at the centre of things even when life seems crazy? The throne! Nothing is unnoticed by the one enthroned upon it; nothing can slip past it; nothing happens without its permission; all things will come under it at the end.

The second conviction is this:

The King's throne is based on righteousness and justice

This was certainly not how things looked in John's time! But Revelation resounds with the truth that God's righteousness and justice *will* be seen. The angels will sing about it (Revelation 15:3-4), the multitudes of heaven will shout about it (Revelation 19:1-2), and all will be brought to account before it (Revelation 20:11-15).

The psalmist had summed it up centuries earlier like this: "Righteousness and justice are the foundation of your throne" (Psalm 89:14). This truth that God is righteous and just runs throughout the Scriptures. It is why Abraham could appeal to God with the words, "Will not the Judge of all the earth do right?" (Genesis 18:25); it is why God could make moral demands of his people, as he did in the Law; it is why Jesus could tell the parable of the persistent widow (Luke 18:1-8), showing that if even a godless judge would give justice, how much more will our Father in heaven do so; it is why Paul could base his argument in Romans on the righteousness of God.

Everything about God's throne is righteousness and justice! This is why we should be pursuers of righteousness and justice in our own life and in the world around us. It is why we can appeal to God for righteousness to be seen in specific situations. It is why we make our stand against corruption, bribery and the 'little office schemes'. The throne demands righteousness – in everything!

The King's throne rules everything

Many Christians are spiritual schizophrenics! As we said earlier, they have a dualistic view of the world, in which God and Satan are locked into a fierce struggle, the outcome of which is rather touch-and-go, but in which God will be the ultimate victor because of the cross. Such a view generally believes that the world now belongs to Satan; legal ownership of it passed to him when mankind fell, so the story goes, and God's task is now to wrest it back from his wicked hands.

But this view reduces God to a somewhat impotent and absent deity – and an unjust one at that! It was not *the world* that fell, but *mankind*; it is not *the world* that needs rescuing, but *mankind*. True, the world has shared in the consequences of mankind's judgment (Genesis 3:17) and is horribly spoilt as a result of this, so much so that it is groaning as it waits for its redemption at Christ's return (Romans 8:19-21); but God did not abandon the created order because of that. Indeed, the Bible shouts out loud with the message that, "The earth is the LORD's, and everything in it; the world, and all who live in it, for he founded it upon the seas and established it upon the waters" (Psalm 24:1-2). It *is* his by right, not *will be* his by redemption. When the Bible says that the devil is the "prince of this world" (John 12:31; 16:11), it does not mean he owns it, nor that he has the right to rule it; he is only a usurper; a thief (John 10:10) and a liar (John 8:44). He is prince of 'this world' in the New Testament sense of 'this present world order'; that is, people, systems, structures, and empires, who live life without reference to God. In rejecting Christ, they have made him their prince; but in reality, he owns nothing and has the right to rule nothing!

It is so important that we grasp this, in the way that John grasped it in his revelation. Otherwise, we will retreat into our Christian ghettos and throw up our hands in holy horror every time something wrong or bad happens, declaring, "But what can we do?" or "Everything will be OK when Jesus returns!" We need to remember that there is a throne at the centre of the universe! And that throne has not abandoned its right to rule all things. That means that we can bring *everything* before it. There is no aspect of life – personal, family, educational, business, social, political, economic, global – that we cannot bring before that throne in prayer and confidently expect God to do something about it.

When I first moved to Oxford from Manchester some years ago, I had to return to part-time teaching for a while. After seventeen years out of the state school system, having been to Bible College and been a full-time pastor over that time, it came as rather a shock to go back! I couldn't believe how much the British education system and standards of behaviour had deteriorated over those years. I had one particularly bad class whom none of the teachers could ever control. David Freeman, the Principal of our King's School, often prayed with me to see the rule of God's kingdom established in that classroom.

I will never forget the day when that rule was applied. The day before the class, I had been calling out to God for him to do something when I suddenly felt a verse come to mind: "He shall rule them with a rod of iron" (Revelation 2:27, KJV). I knew that God had given me the key! The next day, I went into that class, and they were as troublesome and as uncooperative as usual. But there was a moment when I felt the Spirit of God come on me and, rather than simply shout, "Quiet!" I found myself saying, "Quiet! I will rule you, even if I have to rule you with a rod of iron!" The class went instantly silent (probably fearing what dreadful instrument of torture I was about to bring out!). But something happened that day in the Spirit; for from that lesson onwards, I never had trouble with that class ever again; in fact, I became one of their favourite teachers and one of the few who could handle them. (And, in true kingdom style, my reward for faithfulness was more of the same, for the next year I was asked if I would mind having the more difficult classes as I "seemed to be able to handle them!")

Something clearly happened in them; but something had also happened in me. I had understood that God's kingdom authority can be exercised *everywhere*, and that it works. I had conquered my wrong theology that it was only for 'the church'.

The King's throne brings government and peace

That story highlights the final point I want to make here: that wherever God's government is exercised, it brings peace.

Isaiah prophesied of the coming Messiah that he would be called "Wonderful Counsellor, Mighty God, Everlasting Father, Prince of Peace. Of the increase of his government and peace there will be no end" (Isaiah 9:6-7).

Did you see the link there? "The increase of his government and peace". The more his government increases, the more peace increases. Do you want peace? Then get under God's government. Do you want more peace, then get under more of God's government! Do you want peace in the classroom? Bring it under God's government and start doing things his way. Do you want more peace in your family, your finances, your work, your relationships, your future? Bring them all under God's government! Find out what he has to say about these things in his Word, and then do it! Making ourselves accountable to someone else can be a real help in working these things out in practice.

Our response?

We cannot talk about 'kingdom rule' in all these areas, however, unless we ourselves are living under the rule of the King. This challenges our self-will, doing things our own way, disobedience, half-heartedness, and so on. But we will not find ourselves being fruitful in the growth of the kingdom 'out there' unless we ourselves are growing in it first 'in here'. If, at the heart of the kingdom, there is a king, then the question I need to ask is: am *I myself* living under his kingly rule?

A Heart!

All this talk about kingly rule and authority could sound harsh, couldn't it? But that's where our second main point comes in; for not only will you find a king at the centre of the kingdom, you will find a king with a big heart!

One of my favourite passages in the Old Testament comes from the time when Moses went up Mount Sinai to meet with God. To be honest, he had asked a rather foolish thing: to see the glory of God (Exodus 33:18). What on earth was the man thinking of? Even when God permitted him to see his glory, he said he would have to shield him in the cleft of a rock lest he got too much a glimpse of it (vv21-23)! And then it came. I have often wondered what Moses was expecting at that point. Smoke and lightning and thunder? Resplendent light like a million-faced diamond at the heart of the sun? Whatever it was that he was expecting, it was certainly not what he got.

What follows is one of the most important passages in the Old Testament, for it is the voice of God himself telling us what he is like. And this is what it says:

"Then the LORD came down in the cloud and stood there with him and proclaimed his name, the LORD. And he passed in front of Moses, proclaiming, 'The LORD, the LORD, the compassionate and gracious God, slow to anger, abounding in love and faithfulness, maintaining love to thousands, and forgiving wickedness, rebellion and sin.'" (Exodus 34:6-7)

The King has a heart! A heart that is soft and tender towards us; a heart full of compassion and grace; a heart slow to get angry with us when we get things wrong; a heart that spills over with love and faithfulness; a heart that sticks at it with us even when we don't deserve it.

This is why we do not need to be afraid of God bringing his kingly government into our lives, family, church, or nation; for the government is brought with a *heart* that runs right through it.

This too should be what characterises us whenever we exercise that government on his behalf. When I extended God's 'rod of iron' over that school class, it was because I genuinely had a heart for them; when we discipline our children, it should be because we have a heart for them; when we disciple others (and especially when we need to bring some adjustment), it should be because we have a heart for them; when we challenge something in our workplace or in our nation, it should be because we have a heart for them. Authority without a heart is not the authority of the kingdom of God.

A Servant!

But God hasn't finished yet! Not only does the sovereign God of the cosmos show he has a heart, he shows that he has a heart of a *servant*. Here is the amazing thing about the Christian faith: every other religion has its worshippers serving their God; but Christianity has its God serving his people – not out of his weakness, but out of his strength. Our King is a Servant King. Some well-known New Testament passages bring this home.

The first is when Jesus washed his disciples' feet in John 13. Arriving for their Passover Meal, they found the food ready to be served, but no servant on hand to wash their feet after their dusty journey. One can imagine the glancing eyes and shuffling feet as the disciples went through in their own minds which of them should do it (anyone but them, no doubt!) When it was clear that no one was going to do it, Jesus, utterly secure in who he was (v3), took the initiative and did it himself for them (vv4-5). Peter, understanding the incongruity of the situation, wanted to stop Jesus (vv6-9); but Jesus the servant would not be deflected. He did it, and taught them that this was not just a one-off action, but a way of life for all in the kingdom.

"Now that I, your Lord and teacher, have washed your feet, you also should wash one another's feet. I have set you an example that you should do as I have done for you" (vv14-15).

Of course, it wasn't the first time he had taught them about servanthood. On the occasion when the mother of James and John had wanted the best seats for her boys in the coming kingdom, and the other disciples had been "indignant with the two brothers" (Matthew 21:24) – for presumably they had their eyes on the best seats for themselves! – Jesus had said this:

"You know that the rulers of the Gentiles lord it over them, and their high officials exercise authority over them. Not so with you. Instead, whoever wants to become great among you must be your servant, and whoever wants to be first must be your slave – just as the Son of Man did not come to be served, but to serve, and to give his life as a ransom for many" (Matthew 20:25-28).

Paul summed up the servant nature of our King in that wonderful 'hymn' in Philippians 2 which focuses on the person and work of Christ. He tells the church that "Your attitude should be the same as that of Christ Jesus: Who, being in very nature God, did not consider equality with God something to be grasped, but made himself nothing, taking the very nature of a servant, being made in human likeness … " (Philippians 2:5-7).

For many years I mis-read that passage. I had assumed it said that the one who was in *the very nature of God* took on *the very nature of a man*; but it doesn't! Paul says that the one who was in the very nature of *God* took on the very nature of a *servant* or *slave* – in other words, in the culture of the time, the very lowest form of manhood that there could be. This is our God! A servant through and through; a servant whose servanthood took him all the way to a cross.

God rightly commands us to obey him, for he alone is king; but his commands come with a heart and with a servant spirit.

Servanthood should also be what characterises us. God wants us to exercise his rule – in the family, in the home, in the workplace, in the nation – but to do it with a servant heart. God is looking, not for *rulers*, but for *servant rulers*. Is that the sort of kingdom authority that I am looking to grow in? Or do I just like 'bossing people around'?

Chapter 4

The Extent of the Kingdom

Some kingdoms just get too big. At least, that's what the United States government felt about the Microsoft corporation as the twentieth century clicked over into the twenty-first. But there is one kingdom that is growing, that just cannot be stopped, that cares little about competition or anti-trust laws, and that has the avowed objective of taking over the whole earth one day; and that is the kingdom of God. The extent of God's kingdom is mind-blowing; and we have the privilege of being involved in it, of enjoying the presence of the future right now.

An All-embracing Kingdom

There is a certain brand of drink in the UK whose advertising campaign promotes it as the drink that 'refreshes the parts other drinks cannot refresh'. That's what the kingdom of God is like! It refreshes the parts of human life and society that nothing else can refresh in quite the same way, and has the avowed aim of transforming them all one day. The Bible tells us that this kingdom reaches and refreshes –

All life

There is no aspect of life that God's kingdom does not touch. When God is our king, it impacts *everything* we are and do. Some Christians live as though the kingdom only affected the religious bits of life: things like praying, reading the Bible, and going to meetings. But Jesus' discipleship training programme touched on every area of life, not just the religious aspects. He showed people the difference that it makes when we let God be king over our character (e.g. Matthew 5:3-10), attitudes (e.g. Matthew 20:20-28), self-control (e.g. Matthew 5:21-22), finances (e.g. Matthew 19:16-30), responsibilities to the state (e.g. Matthew 22:15-21), faithfulness (e.g. Luke 16:10-12), sexual desires (e.g. Matthew 5:27-30), marriage (e.g. Matthew 19:1-9), relationships with others (e.g. Matthew 18:21-35) – not just over prayer and worship!

We need to be a people who believe that the kingdom affects the whole of life – whether personal, family, social, business, or national. Don't settle for believing that the kingdom only works in *the church*! In the kingdom, *everything* belongs to God; that's certainly how it will be when the kingdom comes in all its fullness, so now is the time to start getting ready for the future by doing our part in bringing all of our life under his kingly rule.

All people

There is no one who need be excluded from God's kingdom, though that's exactly what the religious leaders of Jesus' day wanted to do. For them, there was no room in the kingdom for those who didn't keep their religious rules, and whom they dismissed as "sinners" (Matthew 9:10-11) and "this mob that knows nothing of the law" (John 7:49). Rather than help people find their way to God, they "shut the kingdom of heaven in men's faces" (Matthew 23:14).

But God's kingdom exists for *people* – all kinds of people: men and women, young and old, black and white, Jew and non-Jew. Jesus died for them all.

"And they sang a new song: 'You are worthy to take the scroll and to open its seals, because you were slain, and with your blood you purchased men for God from every tribe and language and people and nation. You have made them to be a kingdom and priests to serve our God, and they will reign on the earth.' " (Revelation 5:9-10) (See also Revelation 7:9-10; 14:6)

If 'every tribe and language and people and nation' will be around God's throne one day, then all should be represented among us right now. That's why the early church leaders refused to allow even the hint of division or racism within their churches, seeing any such thing as a violation of the heart of the gospel. In a world deeply divided by race and culture, Paul proclaimed loud and clear:

"You are all sons of God through faith in Christ Jesus, for all of you who were baptised into Christ have clothed yourselves with Christ. There is neither Jew nor Greek, slave nor free, male nor female, for you are all one in Christ Jesus" (Galatians 3:26-28).

"You have taken off your old self with its practices and have put on the new self, which is being renewed in knowledge in the image of its Creator. Here there is no Greek or Jew, circumcised or uncircumcised, barbarian, Scythian, slave or free, but Christ is all, and is in all" (Colossians 3:9-11).

There is no room for racism (even by default) in the kingdom. It is a kingdom for *all* people. The wonderful thing about having people of different races, backgrounds and cultures among us is, not only does it prepare us for life in the future kingdom, it also challenges our own cultural presuppositions. We all read the Scriptures and relate to God with our own social and cultural spectacles on. So there is nothing like being joined to another brother or sister in Christ, who loves Jesus just as much as you do, but who does things differently. I always thought that prayer had to be done with one person praying after the other, thereby fulfilling the biblical injunction that everything should be done "decently and in order", until I visited other nations and discovered that there were lots of Christians who thought that the best way to pray was for everyone to shout their prayers out loud all at the same time, thereby fulfilling the biblical injunction to "make a joyful noise to the Lord"! I soon learned that the kingdom is bigger than any culture; all may bring an expression of it; but all need gloriously transforming by it.

The challenge to each of us is: do my own life and attitudes reflect all this, and does my own church reflect this, as best as it is able to in its situation? Does a kingdom heart for people – all sorts of people – pervade all that we are and do?

All nations

As we have already seen, the day is surely coming when every government, nation and empire will bow its knee to the King of Kings (e.g. Daniel 2:31-45). But if all nations are to be represented before his throne at the End, then God's kingdom must have a heart to impact those kingdoms right now. That is why Jesus gave us the Great Commission: "All authority in heaven and on earth has been given to me. Therefore go and make disciples of *all nations* … " (Matthew 28:18-19).

It is the nations that Jesus is after, not just one or two repentant sinners! This means that no nation is beyond God's reach, no matter what its political or religious persuasions, or what barriers it might put up. I am old enough to remember when the 'Iron Curtain' divided Europe; when Communism was so opposed to Christianity that it had KGB agents following my wife and I when we helped to lead a young people's trip to Russia and when they completely stripped our bus to ensure we had no Bibles hidden anywhere. At one level, it looked as though such an 'evil empire' (as the American president of the time described it) would never fall. And yet, as God's people on both sides of the Curtain prayed over the years, the political scene suddenly changed, the wall was ripped down, and Communism collapsed in its rubble.

That's why we should never abandon any nation; why we should never say that the '10-40 window' is too difficult, or that Islam is too strong. God has broken through such barriers countless times in human history and can do it again! Because the kingdom is for *all nations*. That's why our network of churches has always had a heart for the nations. And if you haven't got such a heart yet, then the best way to get it is to join a trip to one of those nations one day, because that's what changed things for me.

An All-growing Kingdom

The second thing about the extent of God's kingdom is that it is all-growing; the life within it, because it is the life of God himself, simply cannot be stopped – no matter what we do or don't do. Jesus summed it up like this:

"This is what the kingdom of God is like. A man scatters seed on the ground. Night and day, whether he sleeps or gets up, the seed sprouts and grows, though he does not know how. All by itself the soil produces corn – first the stalk, then the ear, then the full grain in the ear. As soon as the grain is ripe, he puts the sickle to it, because the harvest has come." (Mark 4:26-29)

'All by itself' does not mean there is not work for us to do. There is plenty that the farmer can do; but at the end of the day, the seed grows because it is a seed, not because the farmer works on it or worries it! That's how the kingdom is, says Jesus.

Jesus' parables of the kingdom in Matthew 13 shout out loud with this over-riding message that the kingdom will grow and that nothing can stop it.

- *The parable of the sower* (13:3-9, 18-23) tells us that the sower is generous and the seed is good and growing; so there *will* be a fruitful harvest.

- *The parable of the weeds* (13:24-30) tells us that despite all opposition from the enemy, the kingdom *will* prevail.

- *The parable of the mustard seed* (13:31-32) tells us that the kingdom may have tiny and insignificant beginnings, but that it *will* take over everything.

- *The parable of the yeast* (13:33) tells us that, like yeast, nothing can stop the kingdom once it gets to work until the whole job is done.

- *The parable of the net* (13:47-50) tells us that, even now, fish are being caught ready for the day it is drawn in.

All of this should give us tremendous confidence! Above all, it should remove once and for all any sort of thinking that sees the kingdom as a lost or struggling cause; that sees victory as 'touch and go'; that sees the church as a bunch of battered soldiers bravely holding on until Jesus returns. The kingdom is an all-growing kingdom. And that growth is growth right now! This surely has implications for our evangelism, and for our engaging in it in the expectation of not just sowing seed, but reaping crops; for not just casting nets, but finding fish; for not just "going into all the world" (Mark 16:15), but expecting to "make disciples" (Matthew 28:19) as we do so. In short, it is another aspect of God's passion for "bringing many sons to glory" (Hebrews 2:10).

An All-pervading Kingdom

Any of you who have been to a beach will know what it is like for days afterwards. No matter how much you shake your towels and clothes, you keep finding sand. Sand gets everywhere! And that's what the kingdom is like. Like sand at the seaside, it gets absolutely everywhere. There is nothing powerful enough to keep it out. Jesus' parable of the yeast in particular brings this out:

"The kingdom of heaven is like yeast that a woman took and mixed into a large amount of flour until it worked all through the dough." (Matthew 13:33)

Once yeast gets to work, nothing stops it. God's kingdom is like that, said Jesus. Once it starts working in a particular setting, it pervades everything, and nothing can stop it.

Yeast in everything

How we need to remember that there is nothing that the kingdom cannot invade and influence! It can do its work in our family, our school, our workplace, our church, our town, our nation. Such vision in nineteenth century Britain led the chocolate manufacturer George Cadbury to set up a model village at Bournville for his factory workers, Thomas Cook to set up a travel agency to help ordinary people take holidays, and William Wilberforce to spearhead the fight in Parliament against slavery. Let's not believe the lie of the devil that there are some areas of life that the kingdom cannot touch. If it could cause a wicked despot like Nebuchadnezzar to abandon his arrogance and eat grass like an animal of the fields until he gave glory to God (Daniel 4:28-37), can it not impact your own situation with the same power? Of course, we need wisdom from God to know exactly how to implement kingdom principles into life; but God can give us that, if only we will ask. The trouble is, so many of us just never ask! 'Kingdom stuff' is for church, we drift into thinking, and so miss what God may want to do. The 'yeast' is for everything!

One of the requirements of students at the King's Bible College over the years has been to produce a project on "The kingdom of God and ... " some practical area of life that will be relevant for when they leave the college. Over the years topics have included: The kingdom of God and ... the workplace ... disability ... the art world ... equal opportunities ... transport strategy ... adoption ... occupational therapy ... child abuse ... homelessness ... the prevention of inherited genetic disorders ... management training ... the building industry. You see, the kingdom really does pervade everything!

Salt and light

So, how can we start? My suggestion is that the two easiest places to begin are summed up in the name that brings our family of churches together: Salt and Light. Jesus called us to be both 'salt' and 'light' in whatever situation we find ourselves. As citizens of the kingdom, we can be like salt that both stops the rot and brings out the flavour (Matthew 5:13) and like light that both brings in the truth and exposes the darkness (Matthew 5:14-16).

Doing this does not have to be a 'big thing'. When I returned to teaching part-time for a season, I discovered that teachers had not changed much over the years: no one still liked to wash up the coffee cups in the staff room! I therefore began to do something very simple: I washed up the cups whenever I went to the sink with my own. Hardly a great 'kingdom activity', was it? Yet it was noticed. So much so, that it was mentioned in a staff meeting one day as a model that others would do well to imitate! No one got saved(!), but a little bit of the kingdom had been left around for others to taste. Kingdom salt and light can start small; so never despise the effect of even the smallest things we do. 'Acts of kindness' will often pave the way for something bigger.

At the other end of the scale, the pervading nature of the kingdom means at times having to stand up for truth and righteousness. Even on the day I am writing this, one of our church members is appearing before an industrial tribunal, called to give evidence for the plaintiff against her employer. Her telling the truth could lead to her losing her own job, even though no fault is attributable to her. But as we prayed with her in yesterday's meeting, she wanted nothing more than an ability to be a kingdom woman, who would speak the truth, whatever the personal cost to her.

The church as the agent

But in being positive, let's not get carried away! Throughout church history there have been those who, mistakenly, thought that the church itself can bring about this all-pervading kingdom, or even that it *is* that kingdom. Not so! When we start thinking like that, we are blurring the distinction between church and the kingdom. The church is not the kingdom; the church is simply the agent of the kingdom. The dictionary defines an agent as "a means by which something is achieved". The church is one of the main means God uses for bringing in his kingdom; it is the model of what life in the kingdom is like; it is the training and equipping agency of the kingdom; but it is not the kingdom itself. If we forget that, we either become triumphalists (and soon fall flat on our faces!) or co-ercionists (imposing change, but finding that everything has changed except people's hearts). Let us indeed be God's not-so-secret agents of the kingdom! But let us not think that we ourselves are that kingdom!

An All-victorious Kingdom

As we have seen at several points in this book, the kingdom of God has 'victory' in its very genetic make-up. It simply cannot fail! We have already referred to some of Daniel's prophetic words, bringing God's affirmation on this matter: visions such as that of the rock smashing against the foot of the statue and causing it to crumble (Daniel 2:31-35, 44-45); of the beasts that are slain and that yield their authority to "one like a son of man" (Daniel 7:1-28).

This theme of victory pervades the Bible, especially the New Testament, where Jesus is seen as having broken the power of Satan once and for all at the cross and is now seated on his heavenly throne. An image that Paul uses in Colossians particularly brings out the absolute victory of Jesus. Having stated that at the cross Jesus fully dealt with all our sins, he then adds: "And having disarmed the powers and authorities, he made a public spectacle of them, triumphing over them by the cross" (Colossians 2:15).

The victory procession

The picture that Paul uses here was well understood by his readers, being the picture of a Roman 'victory procession'. As a mark of honour, and to underline the completeness of the victory, a Roman general would be allowed to have a grand procession back into the city. In the procession would be singers and dancers, his soldiers, and – right in the middle – the defeated enemy, stripped of both weapons and clothing, in chains, utterly defeated. That's what Jesus has done, Paul was saying. At the cross, the devil and all his hosts were utterly defeated! They may spit and lash out on their way to their final destiny; but their power is broken and their defeat assured.

What about the set-backs?

The truth is, of course, that despite this 'clinching' victory there are still the occasional set-backs, just as there are in any battle. There are times when we pray for the sick, and they don't get healed; there are times when we plant a new church, and it doesn't 'take'; there are times when we take up social issues, and we don't win. That is the reality of living life in this world; and if you have not experienced this yet, then either you haven't lived long enough, or there is a rude awakening just around the corner.

Of course there are set-backs; but that is the very moment when we need to remind ourselves of the bigger picture: that the kingdom is still advancing and the kingdom is still is victorious; and that the health of the kingdom is not dependent on the health of me or of my church. Perhaps our church plant didn't 'take'; but while it didn't, the kingdom expanded by untold numbers in China. Perhaps the person I prayed for didn't get healed; but while they didn't, thousands of others did; and handled rightly, there will still be things that both of you can learn from the failure and grow because of it. If we will open our eyes, we will see that the kingdom is always, somehow or other, victorious.

Optimists not pessimists!

Complete victory will not be seen, of course, until the end, when Jesus returns. No matter how much the kingdom will expand in this present age (and differing theological perspectives hold different views on that), we will not see the fullness of victory until Jesus returns (1 Corinthians 15:50-57). Nevertheless, we are moving towards seeing that fulness of victory in ever-increasing measure. This means that we need to learn how to live as optimists not pessimists (or 'realists', as pessimists prefer to know themselves!). This means recognising our own human nature at times. I recognise that the natural inclination of my human nature is more towards pessimism than optimism. That's why it is good for me to be yoked in ministry to a man like Steve Thomas who brings a wonderful optimism into everything we do. So if you are a 'realist', find an optimist to be joined to! They've caught the spirit of the kingdom!

Chapter 5

The Principles of the Kingdom

Like most things in life, the way the kingdom grows and operates is more 'caught' than 'taught'. While it is revealed to us in the Bible, we still have to go out and 'make it work' in different life situations. It is not like picking up a repair manual and saying, "Let's follow these instructions and fix the problem"; nor is it like a book of 'case law' that has an example of what to do in every conceivable situation. Rather, it has certain *principles* (the dictionary defines a principle as a fundamental truth or law that makes something work) that we can take and *apply* to the situations of life.

Before we look at some of these principles (which are not given in any order of importance), there is one point that I want to underline. These are not just principles for church life or our personal Christian life; because the kingdom affects *everything*, these are principles that can be worked out *everywhere*. You will always have to ask God for wisdom concerning their practical implementation in different situations; but don't settle for anything less than kingdom principles in *everything*! Because these principles really do work – in the home, in the family, in relationships, in friendships, in education, in the workplace, in business, in the media, in economics, in politics ... Need I go on? If God is king of all the earth, and these principles are those of that king, then these principles must work everywhere. Why not try it and see?

1.   Ruling not Rules

As we saw in chapter two, the very heart of the kingdom is about God *ruling*. This means that the principle of *ruling* should have a central place in our lives. But the key issue is that we should learn to *rule* without *rules*!

Pharisaic religion

This is where the Pharisees stumbled. They couldn't conceive of a relationship with God that wasn't based on *rules*. Originally rooted in what we might call a 'revival movement', the precursors of the Pharisees were desperate to be obedient to God, for it was failure to keep God's law that had led to the nation ending up in exile. When they returned from that exile, a movement developed that was resolved to keep the commandments of God, whatever the cost. And to ensure they didn't get anywhere near breaking a commandment, they set up lots of "hedges" around the commandments. So, rather than have a commandment that simply said, 'Don't work on the Sabbath', they wanted to know what was meant by 'work'; and so a host of other rules were added, making clear that not working on the Sabbath included such things as not carrying a pin in your lapel and not rubbing vinegar on your tooth to get rid of toothache.

By the time of Jesus, these man-made interpretations of the law were seen by many as important as the law itself, and so led to many a conflict with Jesus who refused to abide by them. There is a good example of a conflict over their rules in Mark 7:1-8, where Jesus ends up by quoting from the Scriptures: "These people honour me with their lips, but their hearts are far from me. They worship me in vain; their teachings are but rules taught by men." (Mark 7:6-7, quoting Isaiah 29:13)

What Jesus was saying was that God didn't want their *rules*, he wanted their *hearts*. By and large, conforming to rules doesn't win hearts. In fact, a focus on externals actually allows us to cover up internals.

Ruling from the heart

God wants us to learn how to rule without rules! He wants us to rule – our lives, behaviour, attitudes, relationships, desires etc. – because of love for him, not because a rule book says so. This means getting, and keeping, a soft and tender heart towards him first and foremost; it means putting ourselves in a place of openness and accountability to others where unreality can be 'pricked'; it means growing in responding to the Spirit and his nudges. And we can do this in the world, and not just in the church!

Of course, some of us work in situations where rules are important: teachers, police officers, financial advisers etc. But even here, it is the *way* that we implement the rules of our trade that can make such a difference. As a teacher, I held firmly to the rules of the classroom; but behind them all was the spirit that I wanted to communicate to my pupils: that I cared for them and that they were important to me. Ruling was more important than rules!

To put this a different way: the kingdom operates on the basis of *Spirit* not *Law*. In the kingdom of God everything is "in the Holy Spirit" (Romans 14:17). When we do not operate 'in the Holy Spirit,' all we are left with is self-effort; and self-effort becomes wearying – both for us and for others. The challenge to all of us is to "live by the Spirit" (Galatians 5:16) in both the church and the world. Paul wrote Galatians to challenge Christians who had started out on the basis of 'Spirit' but had ended up reverting to 'Law'. His words for them were strong indeed!

"You foolish Galatians! Who has bewitched you? Before your very eyes Jesus Christ was clearly portrayed as crucified. I would like to learn just one thing from you: Did you receive the Spirit by observing the law, or by believing what you heard? Are you so foolish? After beginning with the Spirit, are you now trying to attain your goal by human effort?" (Galatians 3:1-3)

God wants us to be a people who respond in spirit to the Spirit. As we do so, our focus will be ruling not rules, Spirit not Law, and we will grow and know his blessing.

2. Relationship not Religion

Jerusalem and the Temple were the focus of religion in Jesus' day. All that was wrong with Judaism could be found there, which is why Jesus cleansed the Temple on two occasions (John 2:12-17; Mark 11:15-17). The religious leaders were desperate to cling on to their religion; but in doing so, were blind to the relationship being held out to them by the Son of God who stood before them; so much so that Jesus said:

"O Jerusalem, Jerusalem, you who kill the prophets and stone those sent to you, how often I have longed to gather your children together, as a hen gathers her chicks under her wings, but you were not willing! Look, your house is left to you desolate" (Luke 13:34-35).

Like a mother hen, he wanted to gather his chicks (a highly relational picture), but they were not willing. They preferred their religion to his relationship.

Everything in the kingdom is based on *relationship* – hardly surprising when we have a God who is a three-in-one relational being. Relationship is the basis on which we come to the Father; the basis on which 'church' is built; the basis on which we reach out to others. Without relationship we end up with religion, with duty, with dry structure.

But this is, once again, as true for the workplace as it is for the church. Hence, we should be constantly looking to foster a *relational basis* for all we do and are involved in, for the kingdom is relational by nature. We may be a school teacher, but we will look not just to teach, but to build relationship with the children; we may be a manager, but we will look not just to manage and improve productivity, but to build relationship with our employees (we'll get better productivity that way anyway!); we may be a bus driver, but we will look not just to get passengers from A to B, but to win them with a smile and a cheery word as they get on and off the bus.

3. Feasting not Fasting

"Come round to my place for a fast some time!" Hardly the sort of invitation that most of us would wish for. Yet that was the spirit behind the Pharisees. "Let's all be miserable together!" That's why they couldn't cope with Jesus and the sense of life and fun that he brought. It wasn't 'godly' enough.

In Mark 2:13-22 we read of another confrontation between them and Jesus. Jesus had just been enjoying a meal at Levi's – a tax collector who had just been saved and who had invited his friends along to what was one of the first 'Alpha' suppers to meet the man who had changed his life. The Pharisees (and even some of John the Baptist's disciples) couldn't cope with this 'partying' atmosphere – especially with "sinners". Jesus replied by saying:

"How can the guests of the bridegroom fast while he is with them? They cannot, so long as they have him with them. But the time will come when the bridegroom will be taken from them, and on that day they will fast" (Mark 2:19-20).

Clearly Jesus was not opposed to fasting, saying there would be an appropriate time for it (v20); but the essential nature of the kingdom is feasting not fasting, for it is a celebration of the presence of the king. Imagine your Prime Minister turning up on your doorstep and your saying, "Come in – we've prepared a lovely fast for you!" Of course we wouldn't do that; so why do it for the king of kings?

The kingdom is festive by nature. Jesus described it in terms of a wedding banquet (Matthew 22:1-14; 25:1-13) and a world-wide feast (Matt 8:11-12). The hallmark of such occasions is joy! And the hallmark of all that we are and do as kingdom people should be joy not misery. In fact, even when we do fast, our faces shouldn't look pained and miserable (Matt 6:16-18). Isaiah looked forward to the day when God would have a party with his people:

"On this mountain the LORD Almighty will prepare a feast of rich food for all peoples, a banquet of aged wine – the best of meats and the finest of wines. On this mountain he will destroy the shroud that enfolds all peoples, the sheet that covers all nations; he will swallow up death for ever. The Sovereign LORD will wipe away the tears from all faces; he will remove the disgrace of his people from all the earth. The LORD has spoken. In that day they will say, 'Surely this is our God; we trusted in him, and he saved us. This is the LORD, we trusted in him; let us rejoice and be glad in his salvation.' " (Isaiah 25:6-9)

Jesus proclaimed that the party had begun! The future had started! That's why all we do can be characterised by joy, for the kingdom of God is "righteousness, peace and joy in the Holy Spirit" (Romans 14:17). Of course there are times for sadness and seriousness. But the *essential nature* of the kingdom is joy, not misery. How our churches, how our places of work, would be transformed if that were continually kept as our watchword!

4. Attitudes not Activity

One of the things that many of us find hard is that God would far rather have *us* than have our *activity*. The trouble with activity and busyness is that we can get so caught up in it that we neglect the importance of the heart. And then, when we get busy, we begin to get unappreciative or short-tempered with people. Of course God wants our activity and our serving him; but not at the price of our attitudes going down the drain! Given the choice, God would far rather have the attitude before the activity.

King Saul learned this lesson the hard way when, under pressure of a gathering Philistine army and his own men deserting, he felt he needed to *do something*. But he did the very thing he had been told not to: he offered the sacrifice that Samuel had said he would come to offer.

" 'You acted foolishly,' Samuel said. 'You have not kept the command the LORD your God gave you; if you had, he would have established your kingdom over Israel for all time. But now your kingdom will not endure; the LORD has sought out a man after his own heart and appointed him leader of his people, because you have not kept the LORD's command.' " (1 Samuel 13:13-14)

What God was looking for more than anything else – more than skill in battle, more than wisdom in ruling, more than *doing* anything – was a king who had a *heart* that was after him. When Saul proved he didn't have such a heart, God looked for another man, and found him in David (1 Samuel 16:1-13). David's family (and even Samuel himself initially) would have missed him because he didn't 'look right' or wasn't 'playing the right part' yet; but as Samuel saw a likely candidate for the kingship in one of David's brothers, God spoke these words to him:

"Do not consider his appearance or his height, for I have rejected him. The LORD does not look at the things man looks at. Man looks at the outward appearance, but the LORD looks at the heart." (1 Samuel 16:7)

God does not want our activity until he has our heart first and foremost, as Martha learned long ago (Luke 10:38-42). It was a lesson that God once painfully taught me through a crash in my newly-acquired car. It was late one Friday night, and I had gone to our church offices, weary at the end of a busy week, to do some last-minute photocopying for a teaching day I was

doing at nearby Basingstoke the next day. As I hurried home in the rain –
bang! I smashed my new car into the side of a 'Black Cab' taxi (which are
rather sturdily built). I was so cross with God! There I was, doing *his* work,
making sacrifices for *his* people the next day, and he let me have a crash!
And in my new car! I was still mad the next morning as I drove down to
Basingstoke. Fortunately for me, a godly wife was at home praying, "Oh
God, please speak to Mike!" As I called out to God in the (now somewhat
less than perfect) car, "Why did you let this happen God?" the answer came
so clearly. It was one of those handfuls of moments in life when you really
know God has spoken; and this is what he said to me: "You're getting busy
again Mike!"

God had had so much of my activity that week and over the preceding
months; but what he had not had, was *me*.

Always remember that, in the kingdom, attitudes and heart precede
activity and work. We have sometimes summed this up in the phrase 'man
before ministry'; God wants *who I am* before *what I do*. That's why, in 1
Timothy 3, in his list of credentials for elders, Paul lists only one which is to
do with ministry ("able to teach"), while all the rest are to do with character.
Character and heart issues are of central importance to kingdom living; and
such a principle will transform any area of life in the world where it is given
the same priority.

5.   Serving not being Served

Whatever our culture or background, we have all grown up in a world
where it is seen as better to be served than to serve; and therefore there is
something in all of us that still prefers to be in charge rather than to be told
what to do. Indeed, in some cultures 'serving' is seen as a demeaning thing
and therefore to be avoided at all costs. What a shock it is, then, when we
discover that this new kingdom we have entered has 'serving' written right
through it!

The mother of James and John once came to Jesus asking for the 'best
seats' in the coming kingdom. ("They're such *good* boys," we can no doubt
hear her saying!) The rest of the disciples were livid when they heard of this
(for no doubt they had reserved the best seats for themselves!); so Jesus took

the opportunity to teach them about the very heart of how the kingdom operates:

"You know that the rulers of the Gentiles lord it over them, and their high officials exercise authority over them. Not so with you. Instead, whoever wants to become great among you must be your servant, and whoever wants to be first must be your slave – just as the Son of Man did not come to be served, but to serve, and to give his life as a ransom for many." (Matthew 20:25-28)

Greatness in the kingdom comes through serving. This is not something that sits easily with us, but is something that we must constantly give ourselves to. In the church, no matter what 'position' we might hold, we never get too 'big' to serve. Leaders can put away the chairs and clean up the mess as well as anyone else! In the workplace a Managing Director can adopt a servant spirit by the very way he deals with his staff. The minute any of us starts to think, "That is beneath me," then the kingdom is not in our thinking.

The supreme model for us here, of course, is Jesus himself. Paul tells us about his servanthood in Philippians and commands us to imitate it:

"Your attitude should be the same as that of Christ Jesus: Who, being in very nature God, did not consider equality with God something to be grasped, but made himself nothing, taking the very nature of *a servant*, being made in human likeness. And being found in appearance as a man, he humbled himself and became obedient to death – even death on a cross! Therefore God exalted him to the highest place and gave him the name that is above every name, that at the name of Jesus every knee should bow, in heaven and on earth and under the earth, and every tongue confess that Jesus Christ is Lord, to the glory of God the Father." (Philippians 2:5-11)

The one who was in "the very nature of God" (v6) did not 'cling on to it' (the meaning of the Greek word), but rather came among us, not in the very nature of a *man*, but in "the very nature of a *servant*" (v7) – the lowest form of humanity in the culture of the time – even taking his servant-obedience to the point of death (v8). What a transformation that was: from the very highest place, to the very lowest place! But that is why the Father could go on to do what he did for him (v9-11), for servanthood releases the hand of the Father.

Wherever we are, whatever we are doing, whatever our responsibilities in the church or in the world, we should look to be a servant, for such is the heart of the kingdom.

6.   Death not Life

This definitely sounds a strange one, doesn't it? For aren't the gospels packed with promises of life? Well, yes they are; but it is *life* that is released only through *death*. Jesus put it like this:

"The hour has come for the Son of Man to be glorified. I tell you the truth, unless a grain of wheat falls to the ground and dies, it remains only a single seed. But if it dies, it produces many seeds. The man who loves his life will lose it, while the man who hates his life in this world will keep it for eternal life." (John 12:23-25)

A seed that is kept tightly in the hand will remain just that – a seed. But a seed that 'dies', that is buried in the ground, will find it comes to life and bears fruit way beyond itself.

Being citizens of the kingdom means being ready to 'die' – to our own plans and ambitions, for the sake of what God wants; to our own comfort and preferences, for the sake of others; to our own 'ministry' for the sake of the Body of Christ. Let's face it: 'dying' is painful! But there is the promise of Jesus that whenever we respond to this kingdom principle, fruit beyond our wildest imaginings will always come, "a hundred, sixty or thirty times what was sown" (Matthew 13:23).

7.   Choice not Coercion

The conversion of the Emperor Constantine in AD312 was a mixed blessing. Good-heartedly no doubt, he decided that everyone in his vast empire would also 'become Christians'. As many have discovered since – people as godly and well-meaning as Calvin and Cromwell – you cannot coerce people into being Christians or even into living like Christians. The kingdom is a matter of choice not coercion.

In the parable of the Great Banquet (Luke 14:15-24) the master sent his servants out to invite lots of different people to his banquet; but so many of them made excuses: I've bought a field; I'm trying out some new oxen; I've just got married (well, at least this one had some semblance of an excuse!). Putting it simply, they chose not to come. And the master did not force them to. Rather he turned his attention to those who would not normally be invited and urged them to come in instead (v21-24).

At the heart of the kingdom is choice, not coercion. The Son was not 'forced' to come to earth to save us, but chose to do so because he loved us; he was not forced to walk the way of the cross, but chose to do so out of loving obedience to the Father's will (Matthew 26:39-42). Jesus forced no one to follow him, but freely issued invitations (e.g. Mark 1:16-20; Luke 19:1-10), and allowed people to turn the invitation down and walk away, like the rich young ruler did (Luke 18:18-25).

If we are going to be kingdom people, then we too need to adopt the principle of choice not coercion – not just in our own following of Jesus, but in the way that we handle other people. We must never 'box people in' or rob them of freedom of choice. The church is a willing partnership of Christ's people, bonded together through the joints and relationships that God has put between us. We are on a slippery road indeed when we put people under pressure so that that feel they 'ought' to come to our small group or to the Sunday meeting or whatever. Psalm 110 speaks of the *willingness* of God's people: "Your troops will be *willing* on your day of battle" (Psalm 110:3). This is the spirit that God is looking for, and this is what we should look to be and look to draw out of others too. But remember: people volunteer because they have *seen* something and want to follow!

In the workplace too, how much more would be released if a spirit of 'willing volunteering' could be fostered (remember my coffee cups!). We can start by setting the example: offering to do something that no one else wants to do, helping someone to finish off their work when yours is done, clearing up the mess that no one else will – not because we have to, but because such is the Spirit of Jesus.

8. Release not Restraint

Many models of leadership count their success in terms of how many people are 'under them'. (And sadly that can be as true in the church as in the world.) Such models are based on insecurity and the need for esteem. And often, therefore, the person with authority will hold back others for fear they overtake him or even take over his job!

But the kingdom values people above all things, and so sees people, not as a 'commodity' to be used or kept down, but rather as a treasure to be valued and released. Jesus' goal for his disciples was for "the student to be like his teacher, and the servant like his master" (Matthew 10:25). Paul's goal for Timothy was for him to become a mature church leader himself (1 Timothy 4:11-16), not to live for ever in his shadow.

In both the church and in the world, our goal should be to see people achieving their very best potential. As kingdom men and women, we will push them on, not hold them back; we will want to influence, but not clone; to shape, but not restrain. God spoke to me early on about the man who would replace me as the leader of our church in Manchester; he told me to invest in him and that, if I did, he would have 'two' for every 'one' that I had had. To the best of my ability I sought to do that, and now it is a joy to see him taking that work further.

9.   Accountability not Independence

All of us like to 'do our own thing'. But in the kingdom the principle of accountability is very important. When Jesus had finished his initial training of his disciples, he sent them out to 'have a go' on their own; but when they returned they were accountable to him for what they had been doing (Luke 9:10; 10:17). When Paul and Barnabas went on their first ministry trip, it was not because it seemed a good idea to them, but because the Spirit had spoken and the church leadership had confirmed it (Acts 13:1-4). At the end of that journey, the first thing they did was to make themselves accountable for what they had been doing:

"From Attalia they sailed back to Antioch, where they had been committed to the grace of God for the work they had now completed. On arriving there, they gathered the church together and reported all that God had done through them and how he had opened the door of faith to the Gentiles." (Acts 14:26-27)

Accountability is an important hallmark of the kingdom. But accountability can be an external or rather clinical act, unless it comes out of the right heart. The *external act of accountability* needs to flow from the *internal attitude of submission*. Hence, husbands and wives are called to be submissive to one another (Ephesians 5:21), children submissive to their parents (Ephesians 6:1-3), workers submissive to their bosses (Ephesians 6:5-8), citizens submissive to the state (Romans 13:1-7), church members submissive to their leaders (Hebrews 13:17). All of us need to look to be submissive in heart and accountable in action for all that we do, both in the church and in the workplace, for such an attitude is both pleasing to God and helps keep us from the dangers of operating as independent 'Lone Rangers'.

10.   Giving not Getting

The watchword that most people live by these days is, 'What can I get out of it?' The introduction of the first national lottery in Britain produced a sudden and overwhelming wave of 'benevolence'. People were suddenly buying pounds worth of lottery tickets each week because 'it supported good causes'. Of course, the truth was that they were buying them in the hope of winning ten million pounds! They weren't really interested in what they could give, but in what they could get.

Such an attitude is the very opposite of life in the kingdom. Like our God, who did not even hold back his own Son but gave him up for us all (Romans 8:32), we should be those who look to *give* in every situation rather than to *get*. This should be true of when we come to worship (1 Corinthians 14:26-33), when we give our money or resources (2 Corinthians 8-9), when we lend things to people (Luke 6:34-35) – in short, in whatever we do.

The Bible encourages us to adopt an attitude of *stewardship* rather than *ownership*. Stewards know they own nothing; they hold everything on trust for their master, taking seriously the responsibility they have been given and wanting to be faithful in all they handle, for they know they will have to give an account at the end (e.g. Matthew 25:14-30; Luke 19:11-27). Paul's challenge to the Corinthians was that even their very lives were not their own: "You are not your own; you were bought at a price. Therefore honour God with your body" (1 Corinthians 6:19-20).

If we were to live in every department of our lives as stewards and not owners, what a difference to life it would make!

And There's More!

These ten principles that we have looked at are by no means exhaustive. Had we had the space, I would have gladly added others, such as –

* Imparting not insisting (1 Corinthians 1:10; Philemon 8-10)
* Power not prattle (Matthew 7:28-29)
* Confrontation not compromise (Galatians 2:11-16; 6:1-2)
* People not profits (2 Peter 2:15-16; Jude 11)
* Fruit not foliage (Mark 11:12-14).

You can no doubt add more to the list. So many of these things are paradoxes; but then, that is how the kingdom is. In comparison to mankind's ways, it is an 'upside down kingdom'. It tells us to lose our life to find it (Matthew 10:39); to take up a yoke to find rest (Matthew 11:29); to be last in order to be first (Matthew 19:30); to humble ourselves to be exalted (Matthew 23:12); to be a slave in order to be free (1 Corinthians 7:22); to be weak in order to be strong (2 Corinthians 12:10).

All these principles are things that will shape our life in the future; but the future starts now! So now is the time to learn how to grow in them and enjoy them together; now is the time to show to the world that they work.

Chapter 6

The Pattern of the Kingdom

Whenever a new-born baby arrives on the scene, everyone starts to look for the family likeness. "Oh she really looks like you!" one visitor says to the mother; only to be followed by a second visitor proclaiming to the father, "My, she does look like you!" Looking for the family likeness is an inevitable part of life. My wife and I sometimes get out our old photo albums to look back over our three daughters' developing years. The ongoing likeness can be seen throughout the years; but it is a likeness that is also developing in its own unique way.

That's how it should be with everyone in God's kingdom. There should be a family likeness that can be found in us all – the likeness of King Jesus; but it should also be a likeness that is developing and maturing as the years pass by. Paul put it like this: "And we, who with unveiled faces all reflect the Lord's glory, are being transformed into his likeness with ever-increasing glory, which comes from the Lord, who is the Spirit" (2 Corinthians 3:18).

Tourists in Town!

Living in the beautiful medieval city of Oxford, we get 'invaded' by tourists. You can tell the tourists easily: some are wearing their language school's jacket; others are trying to make sense of maps; others have enormous cameras; others have guide books discreetly hidden in their pockets. Tourists stand out a mile! And that's what it's meant to be like with us. In many ways, our home nation is not our home nation any more. Paul, once proud of his Roman citizenship, proclaimed, "But our citizenship is in heaven" (Philippians 3:20). He belonged to a different kingdom now; and so do we.

Once we are born again by the Spirit of Jesus, the family likeness is within us; through the ongoing help of that Spirit, that likeness can begin to take shape and develop; and, like the tourists, we should now stand out a mile as 'different'.

The Family Portrait

So, what is the family likeness? At its most basic level, it is, of course, the likeness of Jesus. I regularly go back to reading the gospels, simply because I want to remind myself what Jesus was like and how he handled himself in life's situations. But Jesus also gave us specific teaching on how we should live as subjects of his kingdom. One of those blocks of teaching is the Sermon on the Mount (Matthew 5-7), which has been described as 'the family portrait'.

In this block of teaching are found some of the key ways of living for God's people. These include –

- Relating to God with heart attitudes that bring his blessing (5:3-12), yet that are the opposite of what the world would pursue or esteem
- Relating to the world as salt and light (5:13-16)
- Relating to the Scriptures with life and not legalism (5:17-48)
- Relating to spiritual devotions without Pharisaic self-righteousness (6:1-18)
- Relating to worldly wealth in a proper way (6:19-24)
- Relating to God's kingdom as the first priority of life (6:25-34)
- Relating to others without being judgmental (7:1-6)
- Relating to God through prayer for all that you need (7:7-12)
- Relating to your own will and the choices that you make in life (7:13-27).

If we are going to grow in the family likeness, then we will constantly need to keep coming back to the family portrait.

The Family Correspondence

Historians love getting their hands on original letters as sources of their history. They reflect so much; not just the facts, but the feelings and thoughts that were going on in people's hearts. That's why the New Testament letters – the family correspondence – are so helpful. Not only do they give us instruction on how to live as the king's family, they reveal to us something of the heart behind those requirements and why they are so important.

Take Paul's letters, for example. While Paul doesn't use the phrase 'kingdom of God' all that often in his letters (just eight times in fact), it is very clear that the kingdom was a central part of his preaching (see Acts 20:25; 28:31). It shouldn't surprise us, therefore, to find kingdom values running through all his letters. They generally start with doctrinal teaching, so that everything we do is rooted in Jesus and the cross, but then go on to apply that for our daily lives. In Romans, for example, he lays out a sound theological base for the Christian faith in chapters 1-11; but then, with a mighty "Therefore" (12:1), he gives the next five chapters over to ethical implications and exhortations. In Ephesians the first three chapters provide the theological base, the second three chapters then being full of down-to-earth advice and commands for godly kingdom living, covering such topics as -

- our place in the Body of Christ (4:1-16)
- the need to watch our minds and hearts (4:17-24)
- the need to stop lying, stealing and arguing (4:25-32)
- the need for sexual purity (5:1-17)
- the need to stop getting drunk, but rather to get 'drunk' with the Spirit (4:18-20)
- the need to develop submissive hearts in marriage (5:21-33), the family (6:1-4), and the workplace (6:5-9)
- the need to be spiritually alert and prayerful (6:10-20).

Whenever you read the New Testament, see these books as both the family portrait and the family correspondence, and ask the Holy Spirit to work into you more of what you see there.

The Key to Change

The New Testament is clear that we cannot bring about this kingdom family likeness by sheer self-effort, however. Only God's divine power at work within us can do that, as surely as God's divine power alone could bring us to new birth in Christ. One sentence used by Paul to finish one of his letters sums up the key for us:

"May the grace of the Lord Jesus Christ, and the love of God, and the fellowship of the Holy Spirit be with you all." (2 Corinthians 13:14)

The grace of the Lord Jesus Christ

What self-effort, trying hard, trying more, being more disciplined cannot do, grace – undeserved kindness – can do. That is not an excuse for sitting back and doing nothing! But rather, for pressing into Christ where grace is found. As the writer of Hebrews puts it, "Let us then approach the throne of grace with confidence, so that we may receive mercy and find grace to help us in our time of need" (Hebrews 4:16). One of the most exciting discoveries I ever made was to find that it was 'grace', not self-effort, that helps me to say 'No!' to what is wrong.

"For the grace of God that brings salvation has appeared to all men. It teaches us to say 'No' to ungodliness and worldly passions, and to live self-controlled, upright and godly lives in this present age, while we wait for the blessed hope – the glorious appearing of our great God and Saviour, Jesus Christ, who gave himself for us to redeem us from all wickedness and to purify for himself a people that are his very own, eager to do what is good." (Titus 2:11-14)

The love of God

It is as we remember how very much God *loves* us that another motivation for change comes. He who loved us enough to send us Jesus will surely hold back nothing from us. "He who did not spare his own Son, but gave him up for us all – how will he not also, along with him, graciously give us all things?" (Romans 8:32). He who loved us enough to send us Jesus will surely not give up on us half way through the transformation process. "He who began a good work in you will carry it on to completion until the day of Christ Jesus" (Philippians 1:6). God has "poured out his love into our hearts by the Holy Spirit, whom he has given us" (Romans 5:5) and will continue to do so until the very end. When we get discouraged by our failure, by our sin, by our weakness (as even Paul did at times, see Romans 7:15-25), it is good to remember that the whole of this kingdom life is rooted and founded in the love of God and that this love never changes.

The fellowship of the Holy Spirit

When Jesus was preparing his disciples for his leaving this earth, he promised to send his Holy Spirit to be to them all that he himself had been while with them (John 14:15-18, 25-27; 15:26-27; 16:5-15). The Holy Spirit still does the same today. That is why it is so important that we are baptised in the Holy Spirit just as Jesus promised (e.g. Acts 1:8) and not just 'born again', for the Holy Spirit is the inner resource for living the life that Jesus has won for us and that Father lays out before us.

And having been baptised in that Spirit, we are then commanded to do two things: first, we are told to "be filled with the Spirit" (Ephesians 5:18) – literally, to "go on being filled with the Spirit". Why? Because we leak! Because it's hard out there in the world! Because we can never have had enough of him! Second, we are told to "live by the Spirit" (Galatians 5:16) – literally, "walk by the Spirit". That is, we are to look to him for his wisdom, guidance, nudges in every situation of life – especially life in the world. It is as we are filled with the Spirit and walk in the Spirit that we will find that we are "transformed by the renewing of our mind" (Romans 12:2) – which is where so much of our trouble begins!

Chapter 7

The Pursuit of the Kingdom

What an exciting place the kingdom of God is! The place where 'the future starts now'! If we have truly grasped what the kingdom is, then pursuing it will become the greatest passion of our life. Opening our hearts to receiving more of this 'future' (and not just by 'waiting till we get to heaven') will be the driving force for all we do. The New Testament urges us to make the pursuit of the kingdom the priority and passion of our life.

The Priority of the Kingdom

In the family portrait sketched for us by Jesus in the Sermon on the Mount, there is a verse that has been one of the key verses of my life – even before I fully understood what the kingdom was all about. I am so glad God showed me it early on, for it has never failed me in over thirty years of knowing him. Having acknowledged the need for things like food, drink and clothing, and then having commented on the worry that running after such things can bring, Jesus said this:

"But seek first his kingdom and his righteousness, and all these things will be given to you as well." (Matthew 6:33)

Make God and his kingdom your priority, Jesus was saying, and everything else in life will always fall into place. My own testimony is that this is exactly what happens; and if you haven't discovered that for yourself yet, then try God out and just see it working! Of course, there are so many other things vying for our priority these days, aren't there? Family life, friends, leisure, work, TV. And some of the voices calling for our attention can be so loud and demanding, especially in the workplace. But Jesus promises that if we will put the kingdom first – in other words, if we will let God come in and rule – then everything will work out fine!

Whatever the Cost

But 'everything working out fine' doesn't mean that there might not be a cost! For this is where faith and trusting God comes in. Settling the issue of the cost is foundational to life in the kingdom. If we don't settle this at the beginning, we will constantly be going back over the same old ground and never making any progress. The moment a problem or pressure arises, we will think, "But did I do the right thing?" So settle the decision at the beginning, Jesus said. This is what the parables of the field and the pearl are all about (Matthew 13:44-46). To get the field, the man "sold all he had"; to get the pearl, the merchant "sold everything he had". It cost them *everything* – but it was worth it!

Following Jesus means taking up the cross, not as an optional extra but as an essential part (Luke 14:25-27). That's why Jesus went on to say that we must count the cost first, for if not we are as foolish as a man who started a building project but who couldn't finish it (Luke 14:28-30) or a king who started a war he couldn't win (Luke 14:31-33).

There is a cost to the kingdom, so settle that issue at the beginning; but again and again Jesus assures us: it's worth it!

Whatever the Sacrifice

Not only is there a cost to the kingdom, there is sacrifice involved in it. The sacrifice will be different for different ones of us, for God has a way of putting his finger on the very thing that has become 'God' to us. When confronted with the thought of sacrifice, some would-be followers of Jesus couldn't handle it: the rich young ruler couldn't sacrifice his wealth (Matthew 19:21-22); one man couldn't face the thought of not having a settled home (Luke 9:57-58); two others wanted to put family life first (Luke 9:59-62); some couldn't sacrifice their traditional understanding of things and so "turned back and no longer followed him" (John 6:66).

All of us face the challenge of Jesus: "If anyone would come after me, he must deny himself and take up his cross *daily* and follow me. For whoever wants to save his life will lose it, but whoever loses his life for me will save it" (Luke 9:23-24). A real cost – but a real promise!

The Future Starts Now!

My first visit to Merryfield House seems so far away now. In many ways, I find it hard to remember what it was like to live as a Christian without an understanding of the kingdom of God. How glad I am that God led me to stumble across the treasure in the field! Over the years, I have had to pay my part of the cost and the sacrifice (not least through seeking to bring a denominational church into the life of the Spirit and the kingdom); but I wouldn't go back on any of it. The pursuit of the kingdom was worth every penny, worth every drop of blood and tears, worth every seed that had to fall into the ground and die.

But that is *my* generation. Those of us from that generation have no greater longing than to see the *next* generation embracing the message of the kingdom, the kingdom in which they have grown up and with which there is always the danger of becoming too 'familiar'. Our testimony is that it was worth the cost and worth the sacrifice. Our heart cry is now: don't settle for a faith that waits for everything until we 'get to heaven'. The kingdom is already here! The future starts now! So over to you to experience even more than we have of 'the presence of the future'! For that is the kingdom of God.